FUN FACTS
EYEWITNESS

SUPER STRUCTURES

Written by Fiona Waters

Illustrated by Celia Witchard

HENDERSON

An imprint of DK Publishing, Inc.

Copyright © 1997 Dorling Kindersley Ltd.

WONDERS OF THE WORLD

Early people found that caves made handy shelters, but there weren't always caves available, so they began making huts instead. Little did those early builders know what they were starting! The world is now full of fantastic constructions of all shapes and sizes. They have been made for lots of different uses, including living, burial, and worship.

THE ORIGINAL SEVEN WONDERS

Ancient and medieval scholars made a list of the seven most wondrous structures in the ancient world. All of them, except for the pyramids at Giza, have vanished or are in ruins.

- THE TEMPLE OF ARTEMIS – This marble temple was built in about 350 BC. Only one of the original 127 columns remains.

- THE MAUSOLEUM AT HALICARNASSUS – This vast marble tomb was built in about 350 BC. The foundations can still be seen and some of the statues are in London's British Museum.

- PHAROS LIGHTHOUSE AT ALEXANDRIA –
  This was built in about 297 BC. At night,
  a fire burned and was reflected by bronze
  mirrors to give light.

- THE PYRAMIDS OF GIZA, EGYPT – These
  pyramids were built between about
  2575 and 2465 BC. It is thought that the
  pyramid of Cheops (King Khufu) may have
  taken 100,000 men about 20 years to build!

- THE COLOSSUS OF RHODES –
  This bronze statue of Helios, the
  sun god, stood at the entrance
  to Rhodes harbor in
  Greece. It was more
  than 110 ft (35 m) high.

- THE STATUE OF ZEUS AT OLYMPIA,
  GREECE – This magnificent statue
  of Zeus, the king of the gods,
  measured 12 m (40 ft) and was
  made of ivory and gold.

- THE HANGING GARDENS
  OF BABYLON – The
  king of Babylon
  built these
  astounding terraced
  gardens for one of his wives.

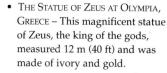

Rocky Dwellings

Early people called *hunter-gatherers* lived by hunting animals and gathering wild plants. They were *nomadic*, which means that they were always on the move, and they used caves as protection from the weather and wild animals.

Rock Temple

At Ellura, in India, there are 34 temples carved into the rocky cliff. Although they are not dwellings as such, worshipers may have spent much of their time here.

Carved pillars inside the Ellura temples

Inside, the rock has been carved into lots of decorative statues and columns, and in places it has been cut all the way through to let the sunlight in.

Cave Dwellers Today

Cave dwellers are called *troglodytes*. In Spain, there is a whole community of these people who apparently think that their caves are more comfy than anything modern architecture can provide!

MULTIPURPOSE

In France, cave homes were carved out of the soft limestone in the Loire Valley. They are now used as all sorts of things, including restaurants, hotels, wine cellars, and even a zoo!

DUG IN THE DESERT

The people of Matmata in Tunisia, North Africa, live in cavelike homes that they dig in the desert ground. These underground dwellings are perfect for desert life because they keep out the heat in the day and the cold at night. (Desert nights can be chilly. Brrrr!)

BUILDING PYRAMIDS

The Egyptian pyramids were built around 4,500 years ago. Each one is a tomb, built by a *pharaoh* (king) as a final resting place for his body. There are more than 80 in Egypt itself, and there are another 100 farther south in the Sudan.

EARLY PYRAMIDS

The first Egyptian pyramids had stepped sides. These may have been seen as a stairway for the dead king to climb to reach the gods and the stars.

The step pyramid of King Djoser was the first pyramid. It was made of six rectangular structures, one on top of the other.

BELIEVE IT OR NOT...

King Djoser's pyramid was only part of a large complex that included a court where the king ran around a track in front of crowds to prove his fitness. Show-off!

King Djoser's pyramid

TRUE PYRAMIDS

Smooth pyramid shapes developed during the reign of King Sneferu (2575–2551 BC). The smooth outer facing was achieved with fine limestone and granite.

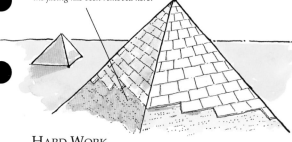

Some of the fine limestone facing is left; the facing has been removed here.

HARD WORK

The ancient Egyptians didn't have giant cranes like modern construction workers. They probably had to shift heavy stone blocks by dragging them along earthen ramps built along the sides of the pyramid.

The Egyptians used sleds to move heavy objects. This may have been how they moved blocks for making pyramids.

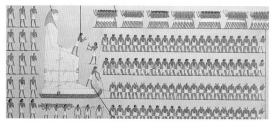

INTRUDERS

Pharaohs were buried with lots of goodies, ready for the *afterlife*, which they believed came after death. Sadly, every known pyramid had been looted by 1000 BC by tomb robbers who were after all the riches.

GREAT PYRAMIDS AND OTHERS

The great pyramids at Giza are probably the most famous pyramids of all. Even the Egyptians thought of them as ancient wonders. These incredible structures were an inspiration to *architects* (people who design buildings) for many centuries to come.

GIZA'S GREATS

The great pyramids of Giza are massive. The biggest was built for King Khufu, around 2550 BC. At 481 ft (147 m) tall, it was made of about 2,300,000 blocks of limestone. Each block weighed about 2.5 tons! Heavy or what?

The smallest pyramid was built for King Menkaura and is only 218 ft (66 m) high – the baby of the group.

AFTER DEATH

After a pharaoh died, he was *mummified* (preserved). The *mummy* was taken to a temple next to the pyramid and priests performed sacred rites on it before it was laid to rest in the pyramid. This was a long, fancy affair.

Mummy case

COPY CATS

Many centuries later, the Mayan people in Central America also built pyramids. These had steps outside and flat tops with an *altar*. This was where thousands of unfortunate people became victims of ritual sacrifices.

PYRAMIDS LIVE ON

Modern pyramids include the Luxor Hotel in Las Vegas, San Francisco's TransAmerica building, and the entrance to the Musée du Louvre in Paris.

TransAmerica Building

Musée du Louvre

The Luxor Hotel

CASTLES

The first castles were built around the 9th and 10th centuries. A castle was the strong, safe home of a lord, who ruled the surrounding land from his impressive accommodation. As the years went by, castles became stronger to protect the lords and their staff from marauding enemies.

A GUIDED TOUR

Castles came in different shapes and sizes depending on where they were to be built, how much money was available, and the likelihood of being attacked. Here is a basic guide to what was where in an average castle.

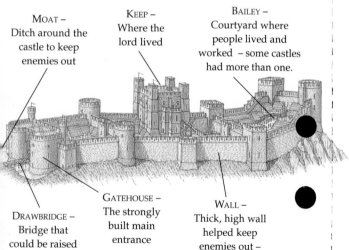

MOAT –
Ditch around the castle to keep enemies out

KEEP –
Where the lord lived

BAILEY –
Courtyard where people lived and worked – some castles had more than one.

DRAWBRIDGE –
Bridge that could be raised or lowered for safety and access

GATEHOUSE –
The strongly built main entrance

WALL –
Thick, high wall helped keep enemies out – some were over 8 ft (2.5 m) thick!

INSIDERS

Here are some of the castle characters you might have met if you went visiting in ye olden days.

The lord and his family were the castle VIPs. Everyone else was there to serve them.

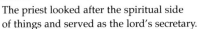
The page was a young servant.

The priest looked after the spiritual side of things and served as the lord's secretary.

The fool provided the entertainment.

A host of other staff helped run the castle and its *estates* (land owned by the lord).

SHOW-OFFS

Needless to say, castles were a symbol of power. Rich families began to show off and competed to build taller and taller towers on their castles. In San Gimignano, in Italy, rival families built 72 castles in the same town! Only 14 of these have survived.

Castle Collection

Castles varied from place to place and from country to country. Here is a small collection of castles from around the world. Imagine what it must have been like to live in one of them. (Dream on!)

Walls for Safety

In the 13th century, it became common to build castles with rings of stone walls, one inside the other, to make it trickier for the enemy to get in. Castles built like this were called *concentric castles*.

High inner wall

Low outer wall

Caerphilly Castle, Wales – a concentric castle

In Spain

El Real de Manzanares

Spain was ruled by people called Moors, from North Africa, until almost 1500. A Spanish castle called el Real de Manzanares (kind of a mouthful) is a good example of the Moorish style. It has lots of square shapes and decoration.

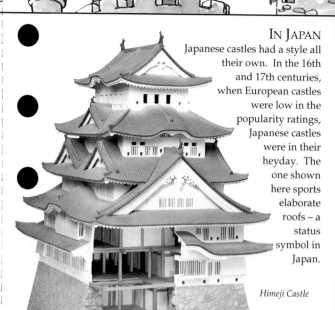

IN JAPAN

Japanese castles had a style all their own. In the 16th and 17th centuries, when European castles were low in the popularity ratings, Japanese castles were in their heyday. The one shown here sports elaborate roofs – a status symbol in Japan.

Himeji Castle

FAIRY-TALE CASTLES

Some castles look like the fantasy homes of fairy-tale princes and princesses. With their numerous towers and turrets, they rise high above the surrounding landscape. A magical, awesome sight!

Neuschwanstein Castle in Germany

TOWERING ABOVE

People have been building towers for thousands of years for lots of different reasons. One of the most common reasons is to adorn religious buildings and give them a look of importance and beauty.

MINARETS AND BELL TOWERS

Islamic places of worship, called *mosques,* have ornate towers called *minarets.* At certain times each day, an official person called a *muezzin* climbs up and calls people to prayer.

Bell towers are another way of summoning people to worship. The 1,000-year-old *campanile* (bell tower) of St. Mark's Basilica in Venice did its job faithfully until it collapsed dramatically in 1902. Whoops!

Minaret

Bell tower of St. Mark's Basilica collapsing

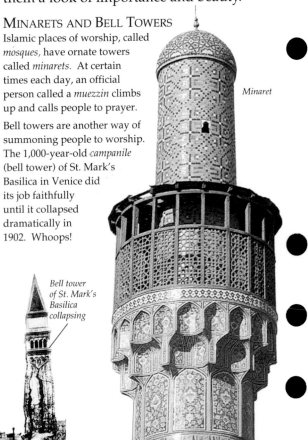

DOMES AND SPIRES

Domes also help draw attention to buildings of importance. Russia's St. Basil's Cathedral has some pretty impressive onion-shaped domes.

Patterned domes of St. Basil's Cathedral, Moscow

Decorative spires reaching toward the heavens were a popular addition to religious buildings.

The Leaning Tower of Pisa, in Italy

LEANING TOWERS

The Leaning Tower of Pisa in Italy was built in 1173 as a bell tower for the cathedral. It leans 16.4 ft (5 m) to one side because of the gradual *subsidence* (sinking) of the ground. Yikes!

Weird Building Sites

Choosing the right site for a building is serious business. The land must be suitable and the finished structure must be easy to get to. However, some pretty weird places have been chosen for some of the world's buildings.

Buildings on Water?

Venice, in Italy, was built on over 100 islands and mud flats in a *lagoon* (a mass of water cut off from the sea). The buildings stand on massive *piles* (columns), mostly made of wood, which are driven deep into the sand and clay under the water.

The houses in Venice are connected by narrow streets, about 100 canals, and over 400 bridges.

Marshland houses are connected by a series of raised paths or roads called causeways.

Marshland Houses

In some parts of America, people live on marshlands because the soil is rich for farming. In North Carolina, the ground has been built up above the water level and a town constructed on top.

BUILT ON STILTS

In New Guinea, an island in the Pacific, coastal houses are built above the water on pillars. This saves land, which is precious because it is used for other things. It also makes it easier for people to get to the ocean for fishing.

Each pillar is made from a whole tree trunk.

NO WAY OUT

Some places are designed to make getting in or out difficult, not easy! Alcatraz, an island off San Francisco, was home to one of the grimmest prisons in the world until 1963. The birds were the only inhabitants of the island that could leave easily.

The island is made of rock and has no natural earth of its own, so soil had to be shipped from another island to make garden plots for the prison guards.

Alcatraz is still an intimidating sight on the horizon.

Special Requirements

Architects have to design buildings to match the function they're supposed to serve. For instance, it's no good to build a railroad station without any space for the platforms, or a theater without dressing rooms!

Industrial Times

In the 18th and 19th centuries, first Britain, then western Europe and the United States, were transformed into *industrial* countries, making all sorts of things from raw materials. This time became known as the *Industrial Revolution* and it brought special building requirements with it.

Factories were built on a grand scale to house huge pieces of machinery.

Lots of people moved to cities to work, and houses had to be built especially for them. In England, the workers lived in long, straight rows of houses.

Rowhouses

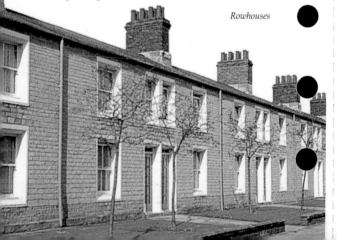

PENGUIN PROBLEMS

In a new penguin pool designed for the London Zoo in the 1930s, slanting concrete ramps made it easier for the penguins to get in and out of the water.

BUILT TO CATCH THE WIND

Windmills do their work by using wind power. Their uses include grinding corn, crushing seeds, and driving sawmills. In Holland they have been used to drain the land to make it good for farming.

Modern windmills called *wind turbines* use wind power to make electricity. These graceful structures are built where they can catch plenty of strong gusts.

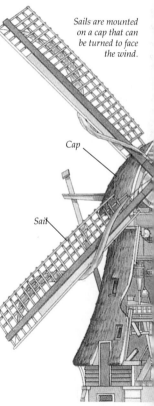

Sails are mounted on a cap that can be turned to face the wind.

Cap

Sail

Wind Turbines

The Forbidden City

 In China, during a period called the *Ming Dynasty* (1368-1644), the emperor Yung-lo ordered the old capital city to be rebuilt. It became known as Peking, also called Beijing. The central part was called the Forbidden City.

Three-zone City

Peking had three zones. The outer zone had houses, stores, and government buildings. Inside this was the Imperial City with lakes and gardens. At the center was the new palace, which was so big it was like a city itself. Only the emperor's family, court, and people on business were allowed in. Ordinary people couldn't enter the city, which is why it was called the Forbidden City.

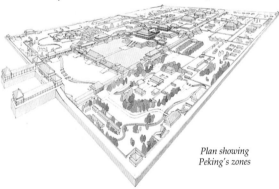

Plan showing Peking's zones

Believe It or Not...

Almost 1,000 buildings form the Forbidden City, including halls, temples, workshops, stables, and a library. There was a throne for the emperor in the middle of each hall.

COLOR AND DECORATION

Color was very important. Pillars and walls were red, platforms were white, and the roof tiles were yellow. Yellow was a color used only on buildings for the emperor.

The underside and edges of the Imperial Palace's roof were decorated with carvings of dragons and other creatures from Chinese mythology.

THE LAST EMPEROR

The last emperor of China was a two-year-old boy called Pu-yi, who came to the throne in 1908. He hardly ever went outside the walls of the Imperial Palace until 1924, when he was forced to give up his title and leave the Forbidden City forever.

ROMAN WONDERS

The Romans were powerful – very powerful! They ruled over a massive empire that stretched from Britain to Asia and Africa. They had vast numbers of people to construct their huge public buildings, including temples, markets, *basilicas* (where courts were held and business was done), and places of entertainment.

THE ROMAN STYLE

The Romans adapted the style of Greek buildings and added domes, *vaults* (arched roofs or ceilings), and large arches. An arch is a strong shape that made it possible to construct bigger buildings.

Roman arches were semicircular.

THE PANTHEON

The Pantheon is a circular temple in Rome. It was first built in 27 BC, but was rebuilt by the emperor Hadrian in AD 120-124. Its huge dome was built by pouring concrete over a temporary wooden framework.
Yes...concrete! The Romans also used this handy stuff.

A hole in the roof called the oculus (window) lets in the sunlight.

THE COLOSSEUM

An ideal day out in Roman times would be to go to the Colosseum. This was an *amphitheater* – a big building used for entertainment and sports. The main purpose of this engineering masterpiece was to provide a place where trained fighters, called *gladiators,* could fight each other to the death. Gruesome!

COLOSSEUM FACTS

- The *arena* (where the action took place) was 620 ft (189 m) across and could hold over 50,000 spectators.

- The arena was covered with sand – to soak up the blood!

- The crowd could be protected from the sun by a huge canopy suspended from 240 poles around the top story.

- There were 80 entrances. The spectators had numbered tickets to show which door they should use.

- A huge chandelier was hung above the arena to provide light for nighttime games.

PLACES OF WORSHIP

Throughout time, people have worshiped their gods in specially constructed buildings. These are very different from country to country because of different beliefs, traditions, and building styles.

A GRAND TEMPLE

Usually, an Egyptian temple was built to honor the gods, but Rameses II built a temple at Abu Simbel to celebrate his own reign (1279-1213 BC). The whole thing was carved out of the cliffs above the Nile River.

The front is decorated with four vast statues of the king himself.

STONE CIRCLE

Stonehenge is a massive prehistoric circle of stones in England. It was constructed around 2,800 BC. The siting of the circle is thought to have had religious meaning for the *Neolithic* people who built it, because its position lets the sun shine through and rise above certain stones.

Some stones were transported more than 134 mi (216 km).

MUD MOSQUES
Mud is used as a building material in hot, dry places. In northern parts of Africa, huge mosques have been built using mud bricks baked hard in the sun. These can even withstand heavy rainfall, as long as the sun comes out to dry them soon afterward!

Pieces of wood support a structure – also handy as scaffolding for doing repairs.

TOTEM POLES
North American Indians made *totem poles* (carved or painted poles). They were symbols representing each family by their crest – a bear, eagle, or wolf, for instance. Some were memorials to dead relatives.

THREE-TIERED TEMPLE
Beijing's stunning Temple of Heaven has three roofs covered with blue glazed tiles. The largest of these beautiful roofs is supported by 12 pillars, each made from a single tree trunk.

AZTECS AND INCAS

In the 16th century, Spanish explorers reached Central and South America and found two ancient and mighty civilizations – the Aztec and the Inca. Both peoples built spectacular cities and temples where they worshiped the sun.

THE GREAT AZTEC TEMPLE

The temple at the Aztec capital, Tenochtitlan, was the center of the Aztec world. Each ruler tried to make a bigger and better temple. It was here that gruesome human sacrifices took place.

A reclining figure called a chacmool held a container for the hearts and blood of victims.

Decorative skull panel

One-way Traffic

The Incas lived in highland or coastal areas and built their cities high in the mountains. These cities had to be built wherever the rugged landscape allowed. One of the most remote is Machu Picchu. There are 143 buildings – 80 are houses and the rest are ceremonial buildings, such as temples.

Big Head

Much of what we know about the Aztecs and the Incas comes from studying their buildings and the bits and pieces that they left behind.

One puzzle is the huge rock heads that have been found. They weigh over 20 tons and stand over 5 ft (1.5 m). They could be portraits of rulers or chiefs.

On the Terraces

Inca farmers built terraces on the hillsides to make more land for growing crops. The terraces also helped stop the wind and rain from wearing away the soil.

BURIAL PLACES

Since ancient times, many peoples have wanted to protect their dead and send them on to an afterlife, complete with riches to ensure everlasting peace. Tombs became more and more elaborate through the ages and could sometimes take a lifetime to construct!

MEGALITHS

Megaliths is the name given to a group of ancient monuments consisting of huge slabs of stone. Early people used megaliths as burial chambers to store human remains.

THE TAJ MAHAL

One of the most famous and most lavish tombs is the Taj Mahal in India. It was built in the 17th century by the

emperor Shah Jehan, for his wife. He wanted her resting place to be more beautiful than any other building. The white marble walls are inlaid with semiprecious stones. Divine!

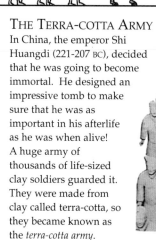

THE TERRA-COTTA ARMY

In China, the emperor Shi Huangdi (221-207 BC), decided that he was going to become immortal. He designed an impressive tomb to make sure that he was as important in his afterlife as he was when alive! A huge army of thousands of life-sized clay soldiers guarded it. They were made from clay called terra-cotta, so they became known as the *terra-cotta army*.

AN ELABORATE AFFAIR

The temple of Angkor Wat was built in Cambodia in the 12th century. It is an elaborate affair, surrounded by moats and courtyards. It is famous for the huge cone-shaped tower at each corner. Believe it or not, it was only discovered in 1860!

THE SPHINX

In Egypt, the statue of a sphinx guards King Khafre's tomb at Giza. It has the body of a lion and the head of King Khafre. It was carved from limestone rock and is the biggest freestanding sculpture to survive from ancient times.

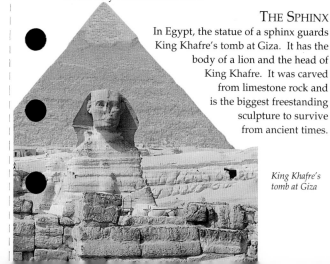

King Khafre's tomb at Giza

BUILDING BRIDGES

When hunters first ventured from their villages, they found that obstacles such as rivers got in the way. The answer? Put a log across and walk safely over. Presto – the first bridges! Today, huge bridges are built to carry people, trains, and other vehicles across water.

BRIDGES OF VENICE

In Venice, Italy, there are two world-famous bridges. The Rialto Bridge crosses the Grand Canal and is the geographical center of the city. There is a shop in each of its archways.

The Rialto Bridge

The Bridge of Sighs, built in 1600, was where prisoners on their way to trial or execution had their last view of the outside world.

GOLDEN GATE BRIDGE

The longest span of the Golden Gate Bridge in San Francisco, California, measures 4,200 ft (1,280 m). It is called a *suspension bridge* and hangs from long steel cables attached to tall towers. The cables are made from thousands of steel wires bound tightly together.

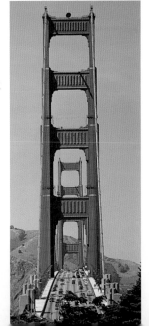

The Golden Gate Bridge

HEAD FOR HEIGHTS?
One of the world's scariest bridges is in Spain. This tiny crossing perches precariously high above a mountain chasm that is some 590 ft (180 m) deep. Heeeelp!

SIDE BY SIDE
The Forth Rail Bridge near Edinburgh, Scotland, was the first major steel-built bridge in the world. The sections are held together by 8 million rivets and balance on huge piers embedded in the river. This type of bridge is called a *cantilever bridge*.

BELIEVE IT OR NOT...
No sooner has the Forth Bridge been painted from end to end than it has to be done all over again! Phew!

GLASS BRIDGES
In San Francisco's financial district, the twin towers of the First Interstate Center skyscrapers are joined together by glass sky-bridges. Don't drop anything heavy!

Natural Materials

The earliest buildings were made of natural materials, including wood, stone, and grass. When people learned to bake clay, bricks appeared on the scene and things began to look up for many builders. Today, buildings are a mixture of natural and man-made materials.

Snowmen

In the Arctic, the Inuit people build temporary shelters called *igloos* from blocks of snow. Apparently, these can be remarkably cozy inside!

Mud

In Syria, Asia, mud houses were made in the shape of old-fashioned beehives. The layers of mud were built up one at a time, with each layer drying before the next one was added.

EARLY CONCRETE

The Romans made concrete by mixing volcanic earth with rubble and bricks. This made a really tough material that is still used today, although the recipe has changed slightly since those early times!

Ovens in Pompeii, Italy – made of concrete

LOCAL TRADITIONS

All around the world, people still live in very traditional houses that have been built in the same style for hundreds of years.

Zulus in South Africa live in kraals – groups of dome-shaped, grass-covered houses with low openings at the front.

The Masai people in Kenya live in long, low houses made from bent branches covered with cow dung. Phewee!

In Switzerland, wooden chalets are built with steeply sloping roofs to prevent too much snow from piling up on them.

Mongolian nomads live in yurts – willow-framed tents covered in felt and canvas.

In Bolivia, South America, Aymara Indians make their houses from woven reeds.

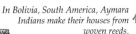

In New Mexico, the houses are built with bricks made from sun-baked mud, called adobe.

ADDED EXTRAS

Constructing fine buildings is all very well, but without one or two vital additions such as windows and staircases, moving around in them could be kind of a problem.

LETTING IN LIGHT

The earliest windows were holes cut into the wall to let light in and let smoke and smells out. If it was cold or wet, the gap was plugged with an animal skin or a piece of wood.

In hot countries, people built very tiny windows to keep the sun out. They did the same in cold countries, but for a different reason – to keep the snow out!

Small windows in India, where it is hot

STAINED GLASS

As glass became more common, windows became bigger, and, by the 14th century, they were vast. By mixing different chemicals into hot, melted glass it was possible to color it, and the stained glass window was born.

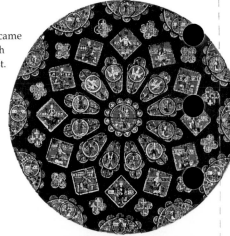

Stained glass in Chartres Cathedral, France

SUPER-MODERN

In the Institut du Monde Arabe, in Paris, the entire south side of the building is made up of metal screens, each containing small "windows" that open and close depending on how much light there is. Futuristic or what?

LONG FLIGHT

Steps are one thing, but the Spanish Steps in Rome are in a class all their own. They link the church with the *piazza* (square) below, but it takes a lot of huffing and puffing to reach the top! Their curves and terraces make them a huge tourist attraction.

IN TIME

Some buildings are designed especially to tell you the time. The clock tower on London's Houses of Parliament holds a 14 ton bell, known as Big Ben, with chimes that are broadcast daily on the radio.

The gold-and-blue clock face on the clock tower in Venice's Piazza San Marco shows the phases of the Moon and the zodiac.

WALLS, CEILINGS & ROOFS

Walls and roofs are absolute essentials for most buildings...but why be dull? Here are some of the world's finest examples for you to marvel at.

ROOFTOP WONDER

Until the invention of flying machines, only birds could see some of the world's most beautiful rooftops. The roof of the Stephansdom in Vienna, shown below, is covered with over a quarter of a million glazed tiles. It had to be restored after it was damaged in World War II.

Just take a look at these stunning tiles from around the world.

France   *Nevada, US*   *Germany*

A Long Job

Between 1508 and 1512, Italian artist Michelangelo painted the ceiling of the Vatican Palace's Sistine Chapel. He didn't just slap on some paint...oh no! He painted elaborate Bible scenes, and it took him four years, lying on specially designed scaffolding, to do it!

Flimsy Walls

Traditional buildings in Japan are made on wooden frames with overhanging roofs. The floor area is divided into rooms by using movable screens covered in paper.

The Biggest Wall

This wall is a special case! The Great Wall of China does not involve a whole building. It was constructed in the 3rd century BC by the emperor to help defend his lands. It stretches for over 1,500 mi (2,400 km), and can be seen from space. That's some building project!

SCRAPING THE SKY

When building space in some big cities became difficult to find, there seemed to be an obvious answer – build upward! *Skyscrapers* was the name given to those tall buildings that towered over the city below.

THE FIRST SKYSCRAPERS

In the 19th century, people began constructing very tall buildings with iron and steel frames. The first skyscraper was built in 1883 and was ten stories high.

A HEAD FOR HEIGHTS

Most of the construction workers employed to work on New York's early skyscrapers were Mohawk Indians. Only a handful of men were hired at first, and they taught their relatives to "walk the high steel."

BUILDING REGULATIONS

As buildings became taller, the streets below became darker, so regulations were made to prevent cities from becoming gloomy places. When a building reached 125 ft (38 m) high, the next part had to be stepped back, and at the thirtieth story it had to be stepped back again. The end result was a building that looked a lot like a tiered wedding cake!

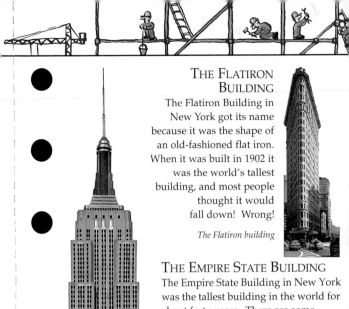

THE FLATIRON BUILDING

The Flatiron Building in New York got its name because it was the shape of an old-fashioned flat iron. When it was built in 1902 it was the world's tallest building, and most people thought it would fall down! Wrong!

The Flatiron building

THE EMPIRE STATE BUILDING

The Empire State Building in New York was the tallest building in the world for about forty years. There are some awesome facts attached to this mighty construction.

- It has 73 elevators and more than 6,000 windows!

- It has been struck by lightning many times – once nine times in 20 minutes.

- The top floor sways up to 3 ft (1 m) in strong winds!

- Because of strange wind currents that move around the building, snow blows up, instead of falling down outside the windows!

SPECTACULAR SPECTACLES

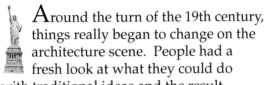

Around the turn of the 19th century, things really began to change on the architecture scene. People had a fresh look at what they could do with traditional ideas and the result was some pretty amazing buildings.

Her torch was to be used as a lighthouse, but the light was too weak.

WELCOME TO THE NEW LAND!

For over a hundred years, a very spectacular lady has welcomed travelers to New York. She is the Statue of Liberty – a gift from the people of France to the people of the United States. She stands in the entrance to the harbor.

- She weighs 204 tons and is 305 ft (93 m) tall from her base to the tip of her torch.

- Her face is 10 ft (3 m) from ear to ear, and her nose is over 3 ft (1 m) long!

- There is a door at her foot leading inside, and there are 354 steps leading up to the observation platform in her crown.

- The seven spikes of her crown represent the seven seas and seven continents of the world.

EIFFEL TOWER

Paris's famous Eiffel Tower was originally built as the entrance to the Paris Exhibition of 1889. At the time it was not liked by everyone and was described as "the shame of Paris," but now it is one of the world's great tourist attractions. How wrong can you be! It is made up of 18,038 wrought iron pieces and on a hot day it becomes slightly taller as it expands!

THE REAL MASTERPIECE?

The Guggenheim Museum in New York houses one of the world's best modern art collections, but the building itself is a work of art, too. It looks like a giant shell and at dusk it is lit up with purple light. It was designed so that people start at the top of the building and walk down in a great spiral to look at the exhibits.

The museum was designed by Frank Lloyd Wright.

INTO THE FUTURE

 New building materials and improved techniques have led to exciting designs. Some seem to soar through the air, defying gravity.

MUSICAL SHELLS

The Sydney Opera House is one of the world's most spectacular buildings. Under the shells that form the roof there are four main halls, two main restaurants, and 60 performers' dressing rooms! The building is surrounded on three sides by water and the roof is covered with over a million gleaming tiles.

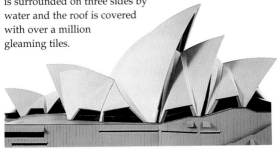

OUTSIDE PLUMBING

The Pompidou Center in Paris looks like an inside-out building! The architects decided to put the elevators, escalators, air and water ducts, and even the steel "skeleton" on the outside.

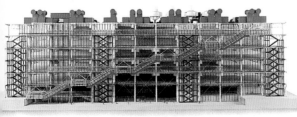

ALL-AROUND EXPERIENCE
Paris is also home to another remarkable modern building. La Géode is a huge cinema with a 11,000 sq ft (1,000 sq m) dome-shaped screen that creates amazing visual and sound effects.

GIANT SAUCER
Brazil's capital, Brasilia, has many modern buildings. The giant "saucer" of its Chamber of Deputies is a reversed dome.

OUT OF THIS WORLD
The ingenious architect Antonio Gaudí designed many fantastic buildings for his native city of Barcelona, in Spain. The buildings are full of curves and many of them are decorated with stunning mosaics.

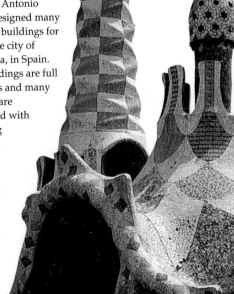

What Next?

So where do we go from here? There are some ultra-modern buildings scattered around the world, and there are plans underway to build more. Some of these ideas may seem like dreams at the moment, but fantasy can become reality!

Sealed In

Biosphere II is a building in Arizona constructed as an experiment. Scientists wanted to explore ways that people could survive on other planets, so the glass and steel building had to be completely sealed and have its own artificial *atmosphere* (air and climate). The idea was that people inside could survive without anything from the outside world.

Fly into the Future

How about this for a building project – a sophisticated airport in Japan, constructed on an artificially built island in Osaka Bay, Japan? The terminal had to be made strong enough to withstand earthquakes and typhoon winds, and large enough to take millions of passengers a year.

COMING SOON...

- The Millennium Tower in Tokyo will be 2,515 ft (767 m) tall.

- Computers will control devices to protect buildings from earthquakes.

- Construction materials will be more ecologically friendly and recycled where possible.

The TransAmerica building has been designed to withstand earthquakes.

- Solar power will be used for heating and lighting.

This is what a house of the future might look like.

- Then, there will be cities in outer space. Awesome! The Russians already have a space station called *Mir* in orbit around the Earth. The US is leading an international space station project called *Freedom*.

Mir *space station*

RECORD BREAKERS

We've come a long way from the days when the first people were holed up in drafty caves. Look around and you will see all sorts of wondrous architectural designs. From the longest to the highest, here is a selection of some really super structures.

The tallest habitable building is the twin Petronas Towers in Kuala Lumpur, Malaysia. Including their spires, the towers are 1,482 ft (452 m) high.

The longest ship canal in the world, the Suez Canal, links the Red Sea with the Mediterranean and is around 100 miles (160 km) long!

The biggest castle in the world is Prague Castle in the Czech Republic, which covers 20 acres (8 hectares).

The largest railroad station in the world is Grand Central Terminal in New York, which has 44 platforms.

The biggest shopping center in the world is the West Edmonton Mall in Alberta, Canada, which is as big as 90 football fields!

The longest highway tunnel in the world is the St. Gotthard Tunnel in Switzerland, which is 10.1 mi (16.3 km) long.

Of all of the cities in the world, New York boasts the most skyscrapers - 131!

The highest city in the world is Wenchuan, China, at 16,730 ft (5,099 m) above sea level.

The Great Canal of China, which runs from Beijing to Hangzhou, was built during the 1200s and is still in use today!

The Great Pyramid at Giza, Egypt, may now seem small, but it held the record for being the tallest structure for over 4,000 years!

The largest sports stadium in the world is the Strahov Stadium in Prague, Czech Republic, which can hold 240,000 people.

The country with the longest rail network is the USA, with 149,129 miles (240,000 km) of track.

INDEX

Acknowledgments: (KEY: a=above, b=bottom/below, c=center, l=left, r=right, t=top)
British Museum; Gordon Models (back cover tr); Sir John Soane's
Museum, London.

Picture Credits: Adams Picture Library: 38br; 47; Bryan & Cherry Alexander: 32c;
Ancient Art & Architecture Collection: 8c; Arcaid/Prisma Parc Guell: 43b;
Christopher Branfield: front cover tr; Corinthian capital, British Museum: back cover
tl; Bristock-IFA: 11b; J Allan Cash Photolibrary: back cover cl; 14br; Courtesy
Chinese Cultural Embassy: 29tr; Colorific!/Blackstock/P S Mecca: 38cl; Michael
Copsey: 24b; Comstock/George Gerster: 37bl; Culver Pictures Inc.: 39br; Michael
Dent: 16cr; Chris Donaghue The Oxford Picture Library: 35crb; ESO/Meylan: 45b; ET
Archive/V&A Museum: 37cr; Edifice/Darley: 19tl; /Jackson:15tr; /P Lewis: 18cr;
Chris Fairclough Colour Library: 20tl; Sonia Halliday Photographs/Jane Taylor: 21c;
Robert Harding Picture Library: 9bl; 9br; 36bc; 42tl; 45cr; /Gascoigne: 4cr; /Peter
Scholey: 21t; /Adina Tovy: back cover bl; 25br; Michael Holford: 12bl; Angelo
Hornek: 32b; Hutchison Library: front cover br;1; 6; 23; 28bl; The Image
Bank/Bernard van Berg: 36bl; /Michael Coyne: 17tr; /David Gould: 18b; INAH: 26c;
James H Morris: 33tl; 34cl; Kansai International Airport Company Ltd.: 44b;
MacQuitty International Photo Collection: 5b; Magnum Photos/David Hurn: 44c;
Panos Pictures: 25tr; Pictor International: 16bl; Nick Saunders/Barbara Heller: 26b;
Scala/Vatican Museum: 37t; Tony Morrison, South American Pictures: 27b; Tony
Stone Images: 14tl; 19bl; 25bl; /Charlie Waite: 36br; The Venice in Peril Fund: 14bl;
Werner Forman Archive/Anthropology Museum, Veracruz: 27cl; Michael Zabé: 9c;
Zefa Pictures: 13br; 45cl; /Rosenfeld: back cover bc; 43t.

Additional Photography: Max Alexander, Geoff Brightling, Geoff Dann, Mike
Dunning, Peter Hayman, John Heseltine, Dave King, Neil Lukas, Andrew McKinney,
Michael Moran, Robert O'Dea, Stephen Oliver, John Parker, Tim Ridley, Kim Sayer,
Karl Shone, Peter Wilson.

Additional Illustrations: David Ashby, Joanna Cameron, William Donahue,
Paolo Donati, Andrew Nash.

Every effort has been made to trace the copyright holders. Henderson Publishing Ltd.
apologizes for any unintentional omissions and would be pleased, in such cases, to
add an acknowledgment in future editions.